Felix Wiebrecht

Comparison of the political and social instabilities in Germany, France and Spain in the inter-war period

GRIN Verlag

Bibliografische Information der Deutschen Nationalbibliothek:

Die Deutsche Bibliothek verzeichnet diese Publikation in der Deutschen National-
bibliografie; detaillierte bibliografische Daten sind im Internet über http://dnb.d-
nb.de/ abrufbar.

Imprint:

Copyright © 2012 GRIN Verlag GmbH
Druck und Bindung: Books on Demand GmbH, Norderstedt Germany
ISBN: 978-3-656-34830-6

This book at GRIN:

http://www.grin.com/en/e-book/207392/comparison-of-the-political-and-social-
instabilities-in-germany-france

GRIN - Your knowledge has value

Der GRIN Verlag publiziert seit 1998 wissenschaftliche Arbeiten von Studenten, Hochschullehrern und anderen Akademikern als eBook und gedrucktes Buch. Die Verlagswebsite www.grin.com ist die ideale Plattform zur Veröffentlichung von Hausarbeiten, Abschlussarbeiten, wissenschaftlichen Aufsätzen, Dissertationen und Fachbüchern.

Visit us on the internet:

http://www.grin.com/

http://www.facebook.com/grincom

http://www.twitter.com/grin_com

Compare and contrast political and social instabilities in Germany, France and Spain in the inter-war period.

2012

One of the most unstable period in history was the era between the two World Wars. After World War I Europe faced a completely new status as devastation was a huge problem everywhere after the war and after the loss of three empires, the Austria-Hungarian, the Ottoman and the German empire. Contemplating the political map of Europe shortly after World War I we discern that in 1919 there are only two countries that were no democracy, this is on the one hand the Soviet Union and on the other hand Hungary. Comparing this to the situation of 1939 there is a big difference, because in this year there are only a few countries with a parliamentary government, for example the major powers Britain and France, Belgium, Switzerland and the Scandinavian countries. Two of these countries that changed their political systems are Germany and Spain. I want to concentrate on them in addition to another very unstable country in this time – France and even France was not changing its political system to 1939 the development of those countries is quiet similar.

One similarity that we can see in all three countries is the governmental instability. For instance in Germany we had nineteen different cabinets from the foundation of the Weimar Republic until Adolf Hitler becomes chancellor in 1933. This looks similar in France where we had thirty three changes of Prime Ministers between 1919 and 1939 and Spain even had different forms of government during this time.

In Germany after the first World War a new form of government was established. The old German empire came to an end when it's important personalities agreed on "a revolution from above"[1] ,as

---

[1] Diehl, E., Faulenbach, J., Hesse, C., Klaeren, J., 2003. *Weimarer Republik* [Weimar Republic]. Bonn: Bundeszentrale

Secretary for the Foreign von Hintze said, to try to prevent a revolution in Russian manner.

Looking at the constitution of 1919 is important when analysing why the Weimar Republic failed and how Hitler could become chancellor. The created position of the so-called "Reichspräsident" had so much competences that he can be named as an alternative emperor because he could break down the Reichstag (Article 25), he was able to suspend some basic rights in order to re-establish the public security and order and to govern without the parliament (Art. 48). These articles show that the Reichspräsident was a very powerful man and this might have been a result of distrust towards political parties and the lack of domination of liberal parties in the pre-war era.[2]

In the national assembly that decided about the constitution there was a majority for the Weimar coalition, the Social-democratic Party (SPD), the Christian Party (Zentrum) and the left liberals (DDP), these parties opposed the councils system and the monarchy. However, the political instability began when these parties lost their majority and this already happened in the first general elections.

Since then several different coalitions were formed consisting of at least three political parties in the beginning and later of four different parties but none of these coalitions could survive much longer than one and a half year. Most of these governments did not gain a majority after elections and worked as minority governments, e.g. the cabinet Marx II that was in office from 27th of May 1924 to 15th of January 1925 and only received 31,5% after the general election of May 1924. Building a coalition became more and more difficult over time because the civil parties as DDP, DVP and Zentrum had to acquiesce continually losses of votes. Taking the Weimar coalition as example we recognize that they could reach 48,6% of all votes in May 1928 but only 34,9% in the general elections of July 1932. In contrast to that stands the so-called "negative cooperation of the totalitarian parties"[3] between the National Socialist

für politische Bildung, p.3.

[2] Berg-Schlosser, D., De Meur, G., 1994. Conditions of Democracy in Interwar Europe: A Boolean Test of Major Hypotheses, *Comparative Politics*, [e-journal], 26(3), p.263, Available through: JSTOR <http://www.jstor.org/stable/422112> [Accessed on 9 November 2012]

[3] Diehl, E., Faulenbach, J., Hesse, C., Klaeren, J., 2003. *Weimarer Republik* [Weimar Republic]. Bonn: Bundeszentrale für politische Bildung, p.60

German Workers Party (NSDAP) and the Communist Party of Germany (KPD) which could in fact never come to reality because of the hostility between these ideologies but it points out in which direction the election votes went on in the Weimar Republic.

For instance the NSDAP and the KPD reached 13,5% of the votes in the general election of May 1928 but in September 1930 they achieved 31,9% which is a massive rise.

The other democratic parties did not cooperate properly to secure the democratic habits and prevent further victories of the totalitarian parties. The failure of providing stable coalitions led to the establishment of another way to pass laws, through the Reichspräsident. In this time there were three presidential cabinets which do not have a majority in parliament but if they wanted to pass a law they relied on Article 48 of the constitution as it states that the head of state can govern in form of so-called emergency decrees without the parliament for a certain time. All this led to an extreme political instability in the Weimar Republic.

However, political instabilities were also possible to observe in France and Spain during the inter-war period.

In France we had even a higher number of cabinets during these approximately twenty years. In contrast to Germany the parties in the Third French Republic more often built up alliances before general elections. This was the case in 1919 when the Bloc National, consisting of various parties only excluding monarchists and socialists, won the election. This Bloc National collapsed because it was not able to introduce any reforms, neither in economy nor in pronatalism actions. After that another alliance took over, it was the Cartel des Gauches, a coalition between radicals and the French worker section (SFIO) but the left at this time proved itself as very bad organised and not able to unravel any problems. In cause of this, the former Prime Minister, Raymond Poincaré, was called to make the next attempt to stabilise the political system, and "Under him, the French began to believe that they had rediscovered the elusive tranquillity, stability and prosperity for which they had been searching since 1918"[4]. When he had to leave his office in 1929 France was in

---

[4] McMillan, J., 1992. *Twentieth-century France – Politics and Society 1898-1991.* NewYork: Routledge, Chapman and Hall, Inc., p.96

the middle of the economic crisis and several Prime Ministers failed in finding proper solutions for it and so the governments changed very constantly. The deflation policy was not popular at all but leading politicians did not find alternatives. This development of short-living governments was hoped to be finished when the united Left under the name Popular Front won the elections of 1936 with its leader Leon Blum but he also failed because of the economic problems.

As Thompson concludes the "French democracy and the national policy which it produced failed to meet adequately the social, economic and political challenge of twentieth-century conditions, both at home and abroad."[5]

Moreover we can examine this political instability in Spain, too. In the years of restoration the two main political parties, Partido Conservador and Partido Liberal, agreed on the so-called Turno system which allowed them to alternate in power and this should lead to more political stability. This system could no longer survive from 1918 as there were no longer parliamentary majorities and because of internal divisions the old two party system changed in al multi-party one. These parliamentarian instabilities were abolished in 1923 when General Primo de Rivera came to power and established a military dictatorship which is also called "economic-corporate dictatorship"[6]. However, this dictatorship was only supposed to be the beginning of more political stability and in 1929, when his opposition rose up he was aware of the need for elections. After this phase of dictatorship elections on municipal level were held and the republican-socialist coalition won in all major cities and used this opportunity to proclaim the Republic but in the provisional government there was no shared vision of the new Republic. When the polarization between right and left became too harsh the civil war broke out in 1936.

As the different governments could not solve the various problems of this time many opponents of the republics saw their opportunity to become the powerful man. We have coups both in Germany

---

[5] Thomson, D., 1946. *Democracy in France – The Third Republic*. Oxford: University Press, p.173
[6] Riley, D., 2005, Civic Associations and Authoritarian Regimes in Interwar Europe: Italy and Spain in Comparative Perspective, *American Sociological Review*, [e-journal] 70(2), p.289, Available through JSTOR: < http://www.jstor.org/stable/414537> [Accessed 9 November 2012]

and Spain in this time. For instance we have the Kapp-Lüttwitz putsch and Hitler-putsch in Germany in the years 1920 and 1923 both from the extreme right side of the political spectrum. Furthermore a dictatorship was created through constitutional measures in Bavaria in 1923. There is a comparable situation in inter-war Spain as there were several coups as well but in contrast to Germany there was one coup that was successful, namely the coup of General Miguel Primo de Rivera in 1923 as he staged a riot and was then supported by the king. This dictatorship went on until 1929 but even after then we have several attempts to overthrow the government, for instance on 10th August 1932 were a group of monarchist under General Sanjurjo tried to establish a monarchy and also in the last months of the Republic when the right forces were successful in parts of the country with their coup d'etat which then led to the Civil War.

In Spain there was a phenomenon that could not been observed at this level in Germany or France at this time and it was one of the main reasons why society polarized more and more. It was the strong will for independence especially in Catalonia and Basque-provinces. After the Second World War the question of independence was the main topic in Spanish society. However, it was soon put in the background when the first social upheavals arose.

Strikes, riots and street fights can be seen in France, Germany and Spain during the inter-war period.

In Spain these riots already began during the First World War as the lower social classes were the first to make their anger public and these strikes often ended in violent outbursts. Between 1918 and 1921 the strikes reached an unprecedented level of intensity because their was a uncontrolled rise of violence and the number of strikes but also terrorism became a measure of resistance against the economic situation because Spain faced a high inflation of costs at this time. The protester's aims were predominantly economic as they made demands on higher wages and shorter working-days for instance. The intensity of violation can be proved by the high number of deaths as more than 300 people died because of riots between 1916 and 1923 only in the province of Barcelona.

Influenced by the Bolshevik revolution in Russia the socialists became more radical and to be a counterpart of that all the opponents of a socialism became more radical as well. With the deepening of the economic crisis the strikes flashed up once again and these became even more harsher when the autonomous right party entered the government in 1934. Further the power passed from the parliament onto the streets in 1936 and this was the beginning of the Civil War because both left and right were mobilised and willing to seize power.

In Germany there are also various strikes and riots beginning with the revolution starting on 9 November 1918 with a general strike and resulting in the dual proclamation of the republic by Philipp Scheidemann and Karl Liebknecht. In the first time of the Weimar Republic there were nearly no quiet periods of time as there were the Christmas fights in 1918, the January uprising and the spring riots in 1919 and several proclamations of smaller short-lived soviet republics, there was even a soviet republic proclaimed in Bavaria by the Communist Party of Germany with a red army. When this communist government was abolished it was simultaneously the end of the revolution of 1918/1919 in Germany. After the failed revolution a broad spectrum of right-wing extremist parties arose to be a counterpart to further revolutionary attempts. Until approximately 1924 the republic was constantly threatened from the right-wing and the left-wing. However, between 1924 and 1929 dramatic inner political crises and violent attempts to overthrow the government stayed away. After 1930 political violence was usual also because nearly every party had its own army organisation and the years 1931 and 1932 were characterized by street fights and in some cities even civil war-like situations. In the summer 1932 Germany experienced the most bloody election campaign with over 300 deaths and more than 1100 injured people only in June and July.

These social upheavals can also be seen in France for instance on 6 February 1934 when 30,000 members of anti-parliamentary leagues and veterans demonstrated against the new formed government and tried to invade the Chamber of Deputies and 16 people were killed in a confrontation with the police. In France we can see the phenomenon that the left mobilised heavily to prevent fascism whereas in Germany for example the Communist Party even formed an alliance with the national socialists in Prussia in 1931.

From 1917 to 1920 there is a massive strike wave in France, in between including over 500,000

people but then it was comparable quiet until 6 February 1934. From then on the communists

become more active and clash more often together with the police. The 'social explosion' arises in

May 1936 as the workers' response to the victory of the Popular Front. It was "the biggest

demonstration of working-class protest France had ever seen"[7] beginning in aviation factories in Le

Havre and Toulouse and led to a huge strike wave through all French industries. The strike wave

rises again renewed in the last third of 1936 when the promised reforms are neglected with a total of

2,428 strikes including 295,000 strikers.

In conclusion we can examine that there are similarities and differences in the development in the

inter-war period. There is a political instability in all three countries traceable in the high fluctuation

of governments and the threats of the republics from both left and right. Furthermore we can say

that over time there is more and more a confrontation between left and right, it seems as if the

centre parties are not present in this time and this can be proved with the help of the election results

for instance in Germany where the extreme parties gain more and more votes whereas the moderate

centre parties lose more and more, in Spain left and right fight against each other in the civil war

and in France there were two major alliances in the general elections of 1936. Though there was no

direct confrontation between a united left against a united right in Germany because the hostility

between communists and social democrats was too strong.

Moreover all countries are affected by the Great Depression as it generates major problems like

high unemployment rates and we can see that no party ever in power in the three countries know

how handle this situation best. The deflation policy, used in all of the three countries, worsened the

situation of many parts of the population more and more and so all three countries had to face major

social upheavals, riot, strikes and revolts which often turned out to be violent and led to several

deaths.

However, we can see that in all the countries there was a period of stability within the inter-war

---

[7] McMillan, J., 1992. *Twentieth-century France – Politics and Society 1898-1991*. NewYork:
Routledge, Chapman and Hall, Inc., p.112

period, in Germany it were the 'Golden Twenties', in Spain at least the first years under the dictatorship of Primo and in France the attempt to stabilise under Prime Minister Poincaré. Furthermore Spain's and Germany's governments were threatened by several serious attempts to overthrow it.

A major difference in my opinion between these countries in the inter-war period was that the German left was always divided. This was a big problem in relation to prevent the catastrophe of national socialism whereas in Spain the republicans fought united against the right and in France they mobilised against fascism and united for instance to the Popular Front. It can be said that there was no change in the political system in Germany until 1933 whereas Spain went through democracy, dictatorship and a civil war until 1939.

Another difference between the three countries is the point from which they start to exist. France Spain have already been republics before the First World War whereas Germany had to undergo the transition from an empire to a republic. This, and the several threats from the left and right, caused that the Weimar Republic could never grow together organically.

To summarize one can state that all three republics failed because of the great differences that existed between different social groups and it was not possible to introduce sufficient reforms that suit everyone.

Bibliography

Berg-Schlosser, D., De Meur, G., 1994. Conditions of Democracy in Interwar Europe: A Boolean
Test of Major Hypotheses, *Comparative Politics*, [e-journal], 26(3), p.263, Available through:
JSTOR <http://www.jstor.org/stable/422112> [Accessed on 9 November 2012]

Diehl, E., Faulenbach, J., Hesse, C., Klaeren, J., 2003. *Weimarer Republik* [Weimar Republic].
Bonn: Bundeszentrale für politische Bildung

McMillan, J., 1992. *Twentieth-century France – Politics and Society 1898-1991*. NewYork:
Routledge, Chapman and Hall, Inc.,

Payne, S.G., 1993. *Spain's First Democracy – The Second Republic, 1931-1936*. Madison: The
University of Wisconsin Press

Riley, D., 2005, Civic Associations and Authoritarian Regimes in Interwar Europe: Italy and Spain
in Comparative Perspective, *American Sociological Review*, [e-journal] 70(2), p.289, Available
through JSTOR: < http://www.jstor.org/stable/414537> [Accessed 9 November 2012]

Thomson, D., 1946. *Democracy in France – The Third Republic*. Oxford: University Press

Verfassung des Deutschen Reiches [Constitution of the German Reich], 1919